Fact Finders®

First-Person Histories

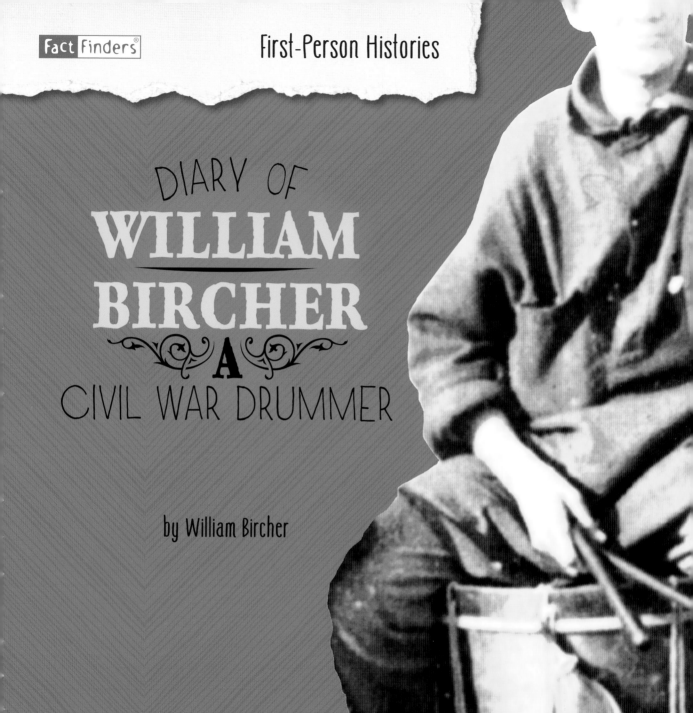

DIARY OF
WILLIAM
BIRCHER
A
CIVIL WAR DRUMMER

by William Bircher

CAPSTONE PRESS
a capstone imprint

Fact Finders are published by Capstone Press,
1710 Roe Crest Drive, North Mankato, Minnesota 56003
www.capstonepub.com

Library of Congress Cataloging-in-Publication Data
Cataloging-in-publication information is on file with the Library of Congress
ISBN 978-1-4765-4195-2 (library binding)
ISBN 978-1-4765-5138-8 (paperback)
ISBN 978-1-4765-5987-2 (eBook PDF)

Editorial Credits

Michelle Hasselius, editor; Bobbie Nuytten, designer; Wanda Winch, media researcher; Laura Manthe,
production specialist

Photo Credits

Corbis: Medford Historical Society, 18; CriaImages.com: Jay Robert Nash Collection, 12, 14, 17; Ebay, 8;
Library of Congress: Prints and Photographs Division, cover (right) 1, 5 (bottom), 7, 9, 13, 16, 19, 20,
21, 24, 26, 29 (bottom, top left); Minnesota Historical Society, cover (middle band portrait), 5 (top), 6,
23, 27, 29 (top right); Shutterstock: Andrzej Sowa, cover (left), B. Calkins, 25, Gualberto Becerra, 15,
Katya Ulitina, cover (hand writing background), Picsfive, (ripped paper design), Veronika Kachalkina, 22;
Timothy Hughes Rare & Early Newspapers, 10; www.thefruitofherhands.com: Jill Howard, 11

Printed in the United States of America in North Mankato, Minnesota.
082014   008409R

TABLE OF
CONTENTS

A Civil War Drummer

William Bircher lived with his family near St. Paul, Minnesota, when the U.S. Civil War (1861–1865) began. Like many 15-year-olds, William was excited about the war. He wanted to become a soldier in the **Union** Army and help defeat the **Confederacy**.

People in the northern states had a different way of life compared to people in the southern states. Northerners said they didn't need slaves to help them earn money. They thought the national government should make slavery illegal. Southerners said they needed slaves to help grow and harvest crops. They thought each state should make its own laws about slavery.

People in the South were concerned Abraham Lincoln would take away states' rights on issues such as slavery. On December 12, 1860, South Carolina became the first state to leave the United States. Ten more southern states quickly followed. On April 12, 1861, Confederate soldiers fired on Union troops who refused to leave Fort Sumter in Charleston, South Carolina. The Civil War had begun.

Union—the Northern states that fought against the Southern states in the U.S. Civil War

Confederacy—the Southern states that fought against the Northern states in the U.S. Civil War

Minnesota officials soon began forming the Second Minnesota **Regiment**. William tried several times to join this regiment, but was turned away because of his age. Finally William was allowed to enlist as a drummer boy.

Many of the 3 million Americans who fought in the Civil War were boys. Both the Union and the Confederacy required soldiers to be 18 years old, but many boys lied about their ages. Other boys like William were allowed in as musicians. The Civil War was the bloodiest war in all of North American history. About 620,000 men and boys lost their lives. Nearly 500,000 others lost limbs or suffered wounds.

William's life was spared, and he was not wounded. But he learned that war is not a fun adventure. In his diary he wrote about the sacrifices, dangers, and hard work of war.

William Bircher in 1864

Union soldiers were attacked at Fort Sumter, as shown in this illustration from 1861.

regiment–a military unit

5

THE Diary OF William Bircher
1861–1865

July–August, 1861—

... I had made several attempts to get into the regiment but, not being over fifteen years of age and small in size, was rejected. But Captain J.J. Noah, of Company K, seemed to think I would make a drummer, as the company was in need of one. I was then taken to the office of mustering-officer Major Nelson and, after being questioned very carefully in regard to my age, was not accepted until I should get the consent of my parents ...

... The happiest day of my life, I think, was when I donned my blue uniform and received my new drum. Now, at last, after so many efforts, I was really a full-fledged drummer and going South to do and die for my country if need be ...

This collection of diary entries was created by William years after the Civil War. In some instances, diary entries are taken word for word from the diary William kept as a drummer in the Civil War. In other entries, William writes about this time in his life looking back as an adult.

Because William's diary appears in its original form, you will notice misspellings and mistakes in grammar. To make William's meaning clear, in some instances, corrections or explanations within a set of brackets follow the mistakes. Sometimes text has been removed from the diary entries. In these cases, you will notice three dots in a row, which are called ellipses. Ellipses show that words or sentences are missing from the text.

officers from the 1st Minnesota Volunteers regiment at Fort Snelling in 1861

October 14, 1861—

... We found the city [St. Paul, Minnesota] ablaze with **bunting** and so wrought up with excitement that all thought of work had been given up for that day.

As we formed in line and marched down the main street towards the river, the sidewalks everywhere were crowded with people, with boys who wore red, white, and blue neckties ... and girls who carried flowers with women who waved their handkerchiefs ...

A poster, created around 1880, shows Union soldiers marching through a city street to join the Civil War.

bunting—small flags joined by a string and used for decoration

Regiment Bands

Each Civil War regiment had its own band. The bands practiced every day and often cheered the troops with concerts. Nearly 40,000 musicians served in the Union Army and about 20,000 served in the Confederate Army.

Though musicians did not fight, drummers did serve on the battlefield. Drumbeats communicated orders to the soldiers, telling them when and how to move. In the thick smoke of gunfire, drumbeats helped soldiers locate their units. Hundreds of drummers were killed as they provided drumbeats in the direct line of enemy fire. Thousands more drummers were wounded in battle.

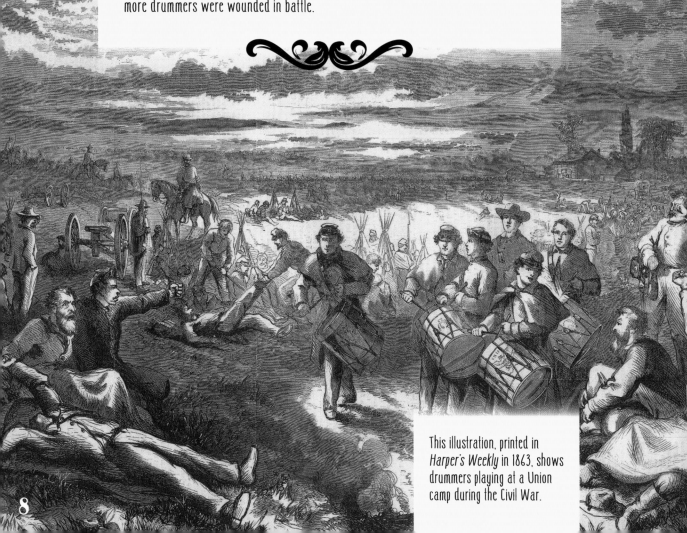

This illustration, printed in *Harper's Weekly* in 1863, shows drummers playing at a Union camp during the Civil War.

January 15 [1862]—

… We made a long march, and at night found ourselves in the wild woods without food or shelter and a long distance in advance of our wagons. Our **pickets** were posted within two miles [3 kilometers] of the enemy. We had a heavy rain the night before, and it had rained at times as we marched …

January 19—

In a few minutes our regiment was ordered on to the field of battle. We marched by the right flank, up the main road, then made a left oblique movement, then regimental front, and double-quick time until we met the Tenth Indiana. Falling back—they having run out of **ammunition**—our regiment charged up to a rail fence, and here occurred a hand-to-hand conflict: the rebels putting their guns though the fence from one side and our boy from the other. The smoke hung so close to the ground on account of the rain that it was impossible to see each other at times …

William's regiment was ordered to the Battle of Mill Springs in Kentucky in 1862. Confederate troops had attacked the Tenth Indiana Regiment at Mill Springs.

This painting from 1862 shows the Battle of Mill Springs in Kentucky.

picket-a detached group of soldiers guarding the troops against a surprise attack

ammunition-bullets and other objects that can be fired from weapons

9

April 1862—

The battlefield was strewn with the wreck and **carnage** of war. **Caissons**, dismounted cannon, and dead artillary horses and their dead riders were piled up in heaps, and the warm sun caused a stench that was almost unbearable ... No historian can ever depict the horrors of a battlefield ... Squads of men ... digging trenches, rolling the dead in, and covering them up with ... dirt, only to be washed off by the first rain, leaving the bones to be picked by the buzzards and crows ...

September 16—

We marched twenty-two miles [35 km]. I had no shoes. I tore up my shirt to wrap around my bleeding feet, which were so sore I could not march without great pain.

Soldiers wore out boots quickly on long marches. A soldier had to keep marching even if his boots fell to pieces. Soldiers from both sides had to take shoes and clothing from the bodies of dead soldiers.

This illustration, printed in *Harper's Weekly* in 1862, shows soldiers crossing the Salt River in Kentucky.

September 25—

Marched to the mouth of the salt river, where it empties into the Ohio [River]. Here we found boys all barefooted, and no shoes to be had. My rags were worn out, and I had taken the pocket from my blouse and wrapped it around my feet; but as it was very thin stuff, I did not expect it would last over an hour or so ... We were furnished with a bountiful supply of bacon, **hard-tack**, and coffee, and we ate as only half-famished men can ...

October 1—

We marched from Louisville [Kentucky] and encamped eight miles [13 km] from Shepherdsville. The country was destitute of water. None was to be had except in pools and puddles along the road, which was very warm and **putrid**. Weather very hot and the roads dusty.

carnage-the killing of a great number of people, as in battle

caisson-a two-wheeled cart used to carry ammunition

hardtack-a hard cracker

putrid-decaying or rotten

January 1, 1863—

... Vandyke and I were the only ones left out of the eleven drummers that left Minnesota in '61 and, of course, we had to do the entire guard duty. While sitting in the guard-tent I figured up the miles we had marched in 1862, taken from a daily account I kept, as follows:
January, 101 miles [163 km];
February, 149 [240 km];
March, 52 [84 km];
April, 158 [254 km];
May, 36 [58 km];
June, 129 [208 km],
July, 39 [63 km];
August 101 [163 km];
September, 258 [415 km];
October, 343 [552 km];
November, 98 [158 km];
December, 29 [47 km];
total, 1493 miles [2,403 km] for the year.

January 8—

Rain, snow, and hail all together made it [camp life] more interesting. Such weather as this knocked all the enthusiasm out of trying to be a hero, and most of us were about sick of the hero business.

Saturday, July 4—

My seventeenth birthday. A salute of one hundred guns was fired—not on account of my birthday—but the birth of the republic ...

Soldiers had to endure harsh weather at camp during the Civil War, as shown in this illustration of Union soldiers at the Potomac River in 1861.

A Soldier's Life

In the fall and winter of 1862, William's regiment continued to march through Kentucky, Tennessee, Missouri, and Alabama. The regiment often fought with the Confederates they met.

William spent the winter and summer of 1863 in Tennessee. During these months, his regiment drilled, marched, battled with the enemy, and endured camp life.

Union soldiers set up camp in Chattanooga, Tennessee, around 1864.

August 19—

Hot and sultry. Marched down the mountain sixteen miles [26 km] into the Sequatchie valley, where we found plenty of peaches, apples, corn, and an abundance of clear, cool water, which we appreciated, as we had had no water since the morning before.

William and his regiment fought in the Battle of Chickamauga in Georgia.

September 19—

Hot and dusty. At daybreak, as we marched along, we saw troops falling into line on the right of the road. The artillery was unlimbered, the gunners stood to their guns, and everything had the appearance of a battle. We marched along the rear of the line until we reached the left wing of the army, where we piled up our knapsacks, formed in line, marched to the front, and deployed skirmishers. We advanced but a short distance in the woods, which was a pine forest, before we came upon the rebel skirmish-line. We heard on our right the heavy roll of musketry and the terrible thunder of the artillery and it came nearer and nearer, until in less time than it takes to describe it, we were engaged with Bragg's army. The terrible carnage continued at intervals all day. At night we heard, from all over the field, the cry of the wounded for water and help. The ambulance corps were doing all in their power to bring all the wounded into our lines ...

The Battle of Chickamauga, shown in this illustration from 1890, was the last great victory for the Confederacy during the Civil War.

The Battle of Chickamauga

In September 1863 William's regiment fought in the Battle of Chickamauga in Georgia. On September 19, Confederate General Braxton Bragg ordered his army of 66,000 soldiers to attack Union General William S. Rosecrans' army near Chickamauga Creek. Rosecrans' troops numbered 58,000. The Union soldiers were forced to retreat the next day, but Bragg's army did not pursue them.

Bragg's decision saved many Union soldiers' lives and allowed them to defeat the Confederate Army at the Battle of Chattanooga the following November.

September 20—

The battle was renewed with terrible slaughter on both sides. Towards noon we heard that Chittenden's and McCook's corps, on our right, had been driven back, and all that was left on the field to hold in check the entire rebel army, was our corps,—[Union General George H.] Thomas' Fourteenth. We held the enemy back until evening, in spite of his desperate assaults, and after dark we retired to Rossville ... Bragg's army was too tired and too sadly worsted to attempt to follow on the night of the 20th.

Union General Thomas' troops fought the Confederate Army after General Rosencrans' troops were forced to retreat.

September 22—

Our band was detailed to the hospital to assist the nurses in taking care of the wounded ... The large business blocks on the main street [in Chattanooga, Tennessee] were used for hospital purposes. We succeeded in keeping the men of our

a photograph of Chattanooga, Tennessee in the 1860s

regiment all together on one floor. They occupied five large rooms, and it was heartrending to see the poor fellows as they were brought in, shot and mangled in every possible way. Every few minutes we had to take one out who had died, and put him in the dead house, where he would remain until there was a wagonload ...

October—

From the 20th to the 30th we did nothing but picket and guard duty ... I was suffering from **dysentery** and found that most of the men were in the same condition. We had no bread of any description for three days.

dysentery–a serious infection of the intestines that can be deadly

Death from Disease

Disease killed more soldiers than bullets did during the U.S. Civil War. Of the 620,000 soldiers who lost their lives, about 390,000 of them died of disease.

William and the soldiers in his regiment often suffered from dysentery during the war. They ate spoiled food and drank dirty water, both of which caused this disease. The soldiers' symptoms included severe diarrhea. Many soldiers died of dysentery.

Antibiotics and vaccines were not available to cure or prevent deadly diseases in the 1860s. But many of these diseases could have been prevented if the soldiers lived in better conditions. Clean food, water, and campsites for the troops would have meant fewer deaths.

Civil War soldiers lived in army camps like the one shown in this 1861 photograph.

Tuesday, November 24—

... We could plainly see <u>General Hooker's</u> troops charging up the side of Lookout Mountain. The heavy clouds, which all day had enveloped the mountain's summit and thus to some extent favored Hooker's movements, had gradually settled into the valley, veiling it at times completely from view. Thus the battle of the afternoon was literally "a battle above the clouds." The enemy was repulsed, driven back from the last position where he could make a stand, and hurled over the rocky heights down the valley.

... Lookout Mountain had been captured, and, before morning, the stars and stripes waved from its peak. The enemy had abandoned his encampment, leaving behind him in the hurry of his flight all his camp and garrison equipage.

In November 1863 William's regiment and other Union troops fought in the Battle of Chattanooga in Tennessee. Union General Joseph Hooker's troops captured Lookout Mountain while Union General Thomas' troops stormed Missionary Ridge.

This illustration shows the Battle of Lookout Mountain, where Union General Hooker and his troops defeated Confederate General Bragg's army in 1863.

General Thomas led his troops, including William's regiment, to victory at the Battle of Missionary Ridge, as shown in this illustration from 1886.

November 25 [Missionary Ridge]—

... From the position we occupied we could see every movement of the enemy ... and they were watching every move we made. We stood in line patiently waiting for the signal to advance. We had not long to wait, however, for at 4:30 P.M. ... the entire army moved as one man ... towards the first line of works, which we soon reached, and drove the rebels out.

... The troops followed the fleeing rebels up the ridge and charged over the second line of works. Here our regiment captured a rebel battery. After the capture of this line, we had but little fighting. The rebel army was routed and fled ... in great disorder. We **bivouacked** on the battlefield for the night and felt that, under General Grant, we had regained what we had lost under General Rosecrans ...

bivouack—to camp temporarily in an unsheltered area

December 1—

We had a grand review. Generals Grant, Thomas, Hunter, and Reynolds, and a score of brigadier generals were present. After the review Colonel Bishop had inspection of regiment. Everything but our clothing was inspected. It was getting to be a serious matter with us. We had not changed clothing for a month or more, and the men were getting filthy and were covered with vermin. We ... had to remain in this condition until we had clothing issued to us; and when that would occur God only knew.

December 5—

Cold, rainy, and misty. We received a large mail, and of course some papers. We could lie in our tents, under the blankets, and read and pass the time. But we had no rest; the **gray-backs** kept us moving ...

December 25—

Christmas: but how dark, how cold and dreary. How dismal everything was in camp. The band boys had all **re-enlisted** except Wagner and I, and we now made up our minds not to remain out. The others had used every endeavor to coax us in, so we at last consented and were mustered in for another three years.

gray-back–body lice

re-enlist–to voluntarily join a branch of the military again

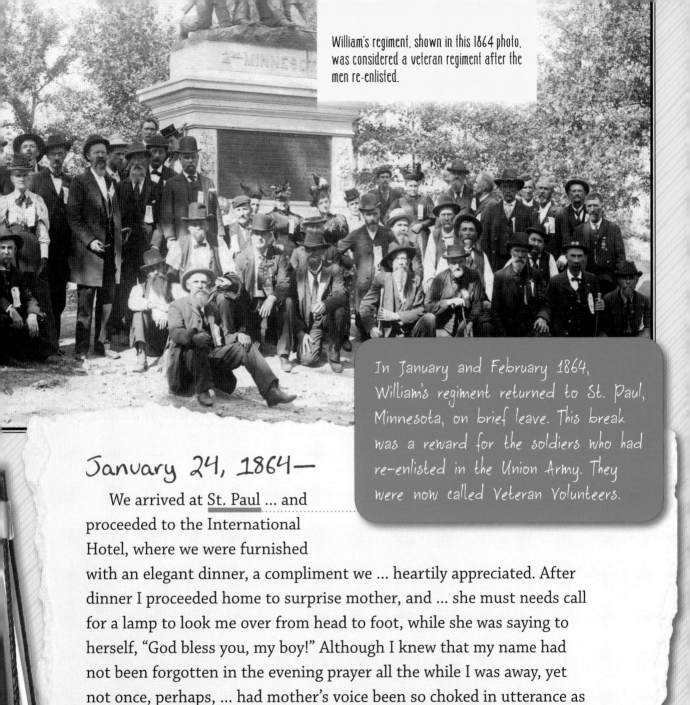

William's regiment, shown in this 1864 photo, was considered a veteran regiment after the men re-enlisted.

In January and February 1864, William's regiment returned to St. Paul, Minnesota, on brief leave. This break was a reward for the soldiers who had re-enlisted in the Union Army. They were now called Veteran Volunteers.

January 24, 1864—

We arrived at St. Paul ... and proceeded to the International Hotel, where we were furnished with an elegant dinner, a compliment we ... heartily appreciated. After dinner I proceeded home to surprise mother, and ... she must needs call for a lamp to look me over from head to foot, while she was saying to herself, "God bless you, my boy!" Although I knew that my name had not been forgotten in the evening prayer all the while I was away, yet not once, perhaps, ... had mother's voice been so choked in utterance as now. With her heart overflowing, she gave thanks for my safe return. When I lay down that night in a clean white bed, for the first time in two and a half years, I thanked God for my safe arrival.

July 28—

... The regiment was in splendid condition and were prepared to undertake and make a vigorous campaign against the enemy. On the 19th we marched twelve miles [19 km] to the Chattahoochee river and encamped.

[October] 26 & 27—

It rained most of the time, which kept the boys in their little shelter-tents. Immediately in front of our camp was the head-quarters of [Union] General Sherman, whom we saw at all hours of the day and night, marching back and forth in front of his tent, with his head bowed, chin on his breast, and his arms locked behind him ... I had no doubt but that he was planning some campaign that would surprise the natives.

[November] 7th—

We made our first appearance with our new silver instruments and created quite a **furor**.

November 15—

Weather cloudy, but warm and pleasant. Marched nine miles [14 km] to Atlanta, and at night we destroyed the city by fire. A grand and awful spectacle it presented to the beholder ...

November 25—

Left the city at 9 A.M. Burnt the bridge over the river at this place. Marched sixteen miles [26 km], crossing the Oconee River. We lost poor Simmers, the drummer of Company G, during the night. The poor fellow, being unable to keep up, lay down somewhere along the road, and was captured by the [Confederate] cavalry that were following us up. I took his blanket and drum to relieve him, but he was too fatigued to follow, saying, "Oh, let me rest. Let me sleep a short time. Then I will follow on." I tried to keep him under my eye, but he finally eluded me, and when we again stopped for a short rest he was not to be found. By that time he was most likely a prisoner. I pitied the poor fellow ...

On November 15, 1864, Union General William T. Sherman began a march through Georgia from Atlanta to Savannah. His Union soldiers burned bridges and tore up railroad tracks to destroy Confederate supply lines. The troops also burned Atlanta and much of the countryside. William's regiment was among the 62,000 men Sherman led.

furor—an outburst of public excitement

Sherman's troops burned Columbia, South Carolina, as shown in this drawing from 1865.

[February] 16 [1865]—

Marched sixteen miles [26 km]. Passed through Lexington Courthouse [in South Carolina]. The troops destroyed every house along the road.

February 17—

Cold and cloudy ... The fences and buildings, the entire length of our day's march, were burning, and the smoke very nearly **suffocated** us ...

In February the Union troops left Georgia and marched into South Carolina. Many Union soldiers blamed South Carolina for leading the Confederate states in separating from the Union. Soldiers destroyed homes, barns, and fences.

suffocate–to cut off the supply of air or oxygen

July 20—

We were then disbanded and said the last "good-bye" to our comrades in arms ... Songs were sung, hands were shaken, or rather rung, many a loud hearty "God bless you, old fellow!" resounded, and many were the toasts and the healths that were drunk before the men parted for good.

On April 9, 1865, Confederate General Robert E. Lee surrendered to Union General Ulysses S. Grant in Virginia. After four years of fighting, the U.S. Civil War was over.

William (front row, third from the left) and the rest of the Second Minnesota Regiment band in 1864

From Soldier to Statesman

After the war William remained in St. Paul, Minnesota. He ran a saloon called Billy Bircher's Place. He married in 1869 and had three children. In the 1870s William became a grocer and began to hold positions in local government. William retired in Florida where he served as mayor of the town of St. Cloud. He died on February 5, 1917, and was buried in St. Paul.

Timeline

Dates in William Bircher's life

Important dates in the Civil War

1861

William enlists in the Second Minnesota Regiment as a drummer.

1860

South Carolina is the first state to leave the Union.

1845

William is born in Minnesota.

1861

The Civil War begins when the Confederates attack Union-held Fort Sumter in South Carolina.

—1845 ‹···················› 1860 —

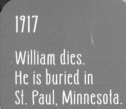

1863

President Abraham Lincoln declares the Emancipation Proclamation. This order said that all slaves in the United States were free.

1864

William's regiment is among Sherman's troops who capture Atlanta and later destroy the city by fire.

1917

William dies. He is buried in St. Paul, Minnesota.

1863

William re-enlists in the Union Army.

1865

Confederate General Robert E. Lee surrenders to Union General Ulysses S. Grant. The Civil War ends.

1863

1865

Glossary

ammunition (am-yoo-NI-shuhn)—bullets and other objects that can be fired from weapons

bivouack (biv-a-WAK)—to camp temporarily in an unsheltered area

bunting (BUHN-ting)—small flags joined by a string and used for decoration

caisson (KAY-sen)—a two-wheeled cart used to carry ammunition

carnage (KAR-nij)—the killing of a great number of people, as in battle

Confederacy (kuhn-FE-dur-uh-see)—the Southern states that fought against the Northern states in the U.S. Civil War

dysentery (DI-sen-tayr-ee)—a serious infection of the intestines that can be deadly

furor (FYOR-or)—an outburst of public excitement

gray-back (GRA-bak)—body lice

hardtack (HARD-tak)—a hard cracker

picket (PIK-it)—a detached group of soldiers guarding the troops against a surprise attack

putrid (PYOO-trid)—decaying or rotten

re-enlist (ri-in-LIST)—to voluntarily join a branch of the military again

regiment (REJ-uh-muhnt)—a military unit

suffocate (SUHF-uh-kate)—to cut off the supply of air or oxygen

Union (YOON-yuhn)—the Northern states that fought against the Southern states in the U.S. Civil War

Read More

Benoit, Peter. *The Civil War.* A True Book. New York: Children's Press, 2012.

Fein, Eric. *Weapons, Gear, and Uniforms of the Civil War.* Equipped for Battle. Mankato, Minn.: Capstone Press, 2012.

Ratliff, Thomas M. *You Wouldn't Want to Be a Civil War Soldier!: A War You'd Rather Not Fight.* New York: Franklin Watts, An Imprint of Scholastic Inc., 2013.

Critical Thinking Using the Common Core

1. Many Union soldiers blamed South Carolina for starting the Civil War because they were the first state to leave the Union. What other events contributed to the start of the war? Use what you know about the Civil War, as well as the text and timeline, to help you with your answer. (Integration of Knowledge and Ideas)

2. On pages 6 and 7, William talks about the excitement of going to war. How did his opinion change as the Civil War went on? Give examples from the text to support your answer. (Key Ideas and Details)

3. William became active in local government after the Civil War ended and eventually became the mayor of St. Cloud, Florida. How do you think being a soldier helped him in his duties as a government official? (Integration of Knowledge and Ideas)

Internet Sites

FactHound offers a safe, fun way to find Internet sites related to this book. All of the sites on FactHound have been researched by our staff.

Here's all you do:

Visit www.facthound.com

Type in this code: 9781476541952

 **Super-cool stuff!** Check out projects, games and lots more at **www.capstonekids.com**

Index